TIME TO QUIT THAT JOB

BEAUTY ISRAEL

Copyright © 2012 Beauty Israel

All rights reserved.

ISBN: 9798351945668

DEDICATION

This book is dedicated to all those who are struggling with their finance and what to make a change by working online.

What you will find inside this book are personal experience on how to scale up from $0 to making $5000 in passive income.

Contents

TIME TO QUIT i
THAT JOB i
   INTRODUCTION 1
MY JOURNEY SO FAR 4
HOW I STARTED MY JOURNEY 6
START AN ONLINE BUSINESS 7
DIFFERENT THINGS YOU NEED TO TRY NOW. 12
HOW TO UPLOAD YOUR BOOKS ON AMAZON KDP 23
THE SECOND ONLINE BUSINESS YOU NEED TO START IS: ... 25
CAN YOU MAKE MONEY WITH A FREE BLOG? 29
GAMING 30
YOUTUBE CHANNEL 31
WHAT YOU NEED TO START A YOUTUBE CHANNEL 33
HOW MUCH CAN I MAKE WITH YOUTUBE CHANNEL? 34
BONUS TIPS 35
HOW TO GET BOOKS TO SELL FOR FREE WITHOUT WRITING THEM YOURSELF 37
   Publish Books Written by Someone Else 37
   Can You Legally Sell Public Domain Content? 37
   How to Find Public Domain Books 37
   How to Publish a Public Domain Book 38
      Pick a Book Title 38
      Format the Book 38
      Create a Cover for Your Book 39
      Convert The Text to the Kindle Format 39
      Finishing Touches 39

How You Get Paid for Your Public Domain Book _____40

How to Sell More Books _____40

How Much Can You Earn? _____41

How Difficult is it to Get Started? _____41

How to Make Money Selling Other People's Products _____42

    Becoming a Sales Representative _____42

    Drop-Shipping _____42

What Is Affiliate Marketing and How To Get Started _____43

    What is affiliate marketing? _____43

    How affiliate marketing works _____44

    Types of affiliate marketing _____45

        Unattached _____45

        Related _____46

        Involved _____46

    Pros and cons of affiliate marketing _____47

        Pros _____47

        Cons _____48

    How do affiliate marketers make money? _____49

    How to start affiliate marketing in 4 steps _____51

        Pick your platform and method _____52

        Decide your niche and audience _____53

        Find your products _____55

        Choose your first affiliate program _____56

UPLOAD OTHER PEOPLE'S VIDEO AND MAKE MONEY _____57

12 of the Best Free Stock Video Websites for Great Footage _____57

TIME TO QUIT THAT JOB

HOW TO MAKE MONEY ONLINE FROM ZERO $

From Zero to Your First $200 Guaranteed

INTRODUCTION

If you are like me that has been looking for ways to make passive income without worrying about pay check to pay check or you simply wants to change your financially status, well keep reading because this is for you.

I'm going to share with you how I was able to make more than 2 million naira in one year doing simple work online and today, it has become my main stream of income.

Well some may say what is 2 million naira?. You know it may sound cheap to some people to make two or three million in less then a year, but to those who have not made even a cent online in their entire life, it means a lot to them.

So on this e-book am going to share with you the exact same

method I use to go from zero to making 2.4 million naira from Aug 1, 2021 to August 1, 2022, exactly one year after I went from broke to having 2.4 million naira lying in my bank account, I now go to the supermarket without looking at the price tag, I just buy and go because I'm sure of the next payment the following month.

Not to talk of the family member calling for money problems now and then, I now sort everyone out because I have the money to do so.

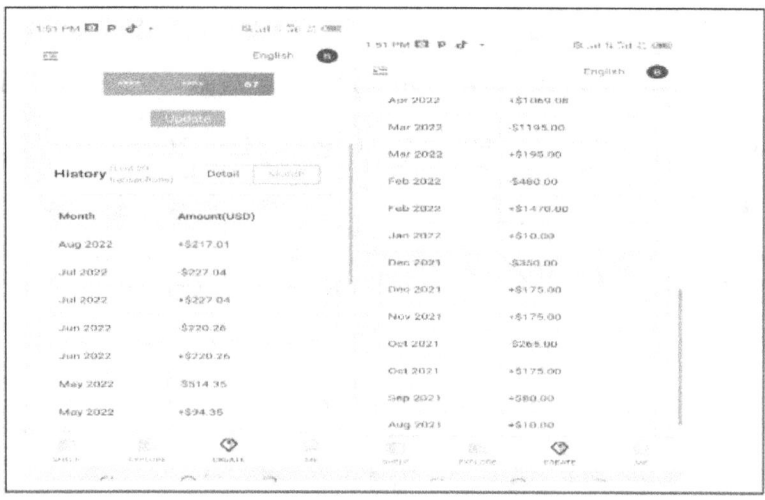

Payment Proof from August 2021 to August 2022

The method and channel you need to use to make this money can not be outdated so don't worry, just follow the steps in this book and you are sure to make money no matter the year you decide to start.

Plus don't worry your head thinking the money is in dollars so how do you get paid if you are from Nigeria, Ghana, or any Africa country?

The money will be converted every month to your local currency and deposited into your local back account. Is that simple.

MY JOURNEY SO FAR

My name is Beauty Israel if you want to know more about me check my YouTube channel, you will see my face and know who is giving you this information.

I'm from Nigeria, and my condition was like every other person who is looking out for a ways to be financially free.

I became obsessed with making money online when I find out that if I didn't do anything about my situation I'm going to go homeless again, well that was not the first time I was homeless and I can tell you it was horrible, it brings tears to my eyes sharing this with you now, so let just leave it at that, let me not bore you with my poverty story as that is now in the past.

This information I'm about to give to you will never fail to produce result, it has taken me from Zero Naira to 2, 427,482.37 Naira and is still counting, the figure I gave on this e-book is what I have make, the best part is it will keep increase every month, it keeps coming every month, and that is what I call passive income.

Now I don't want to start this book if I have not told you that my target is to hit N47,100,000.00 which is $100,000 as at the time of writing this e-book and so far, I have hit N2,429,482.37 which is $6548.45 and we are still in August 20th 2022.

If you want to know how this journey goes, subscribe to my YouTube channel because I will be doing an update of this journey when I finally hit my target of N47,100,000.00.

HOW I STARTED MY JOURNEY

All I can remember is that I woke up one day and had no place to sleep, I remembered staying in an uncompleted building for a year and some months, but before that time I had a good paying job that put roof over my head and food on the table even though the salary was not enough, I still prefer it to living in an uncompleted building.

I find out that crying would not help my situation and begging is not an option since I hate begging. I lost my job due to careless or should I see miscalculation as I resigned to start a business without thinking. Needless to say, the business did not survive the hash reality of the economic of my country, so I lost both my house and business.

So I started searching for ways to make money online, but not just money, I wanted money that will keep coming even while I sleep because I read on the internet that is possible to make money while I sleep. I was so afraid to go broke again.

I was so scared of not having money because believe me is the worst thing that can happen to anyone.

So I came across how I can end my financial woes for ever and that is what I'm about to bring to you

START AN ONLINE BUSINESS

To make this type of money, it means you are willing to start something, because if you are not ready to do something then you can as well forget about making money either online or offline.

But I prefer online money making than offline because in my fifteen years of working for people offline in an office environment, I never had the freedom and money that I now have and to top it all, I now have enough money to pay off my bills and visit some spas that I won't dare to go when I was working for others.

One good thing about online business is that you don't need any capital to start and it is capable to make you a millionaire in your life time.

But you can't say the same thing for an offline business where you have to pay rent, electricity bill, taxes, transportation, etc. Not that you can't be a millionaire with offline business, but I'm talking about people like us who didn't have the capital to even start.

I started my online business with zero capital, all I had at that time was my phone and the determination to make money from home.

And by the grace of God I made my first one million naira in six months with just my phone, no capital, no transportation, no paying of light bill or buying fuel for generator.

With online business you have peace of mind, with lots and lots of money in your bank account and in your pocket.

I can't begin to describe my joy that I now have working from the comfort of my room and not paying a dime in taxes and shop rent.

Now I'm going to take us step by step on how you can start this business and start making those money.

The first thing you need to know is that there are two types of income to work for

1: Passive income

2: Active income.

But the truth is I work for both, the first one I worked for was the active income because this type of income comes once into your account and that is it, I worked for active income for one year before I start working for passive income.

Now if you don't know the difference between the two, let me explain to you.

Active income is the type of income you work for and once you collect your money, you no longer have business with the company, they pay you for your services and say goodbye to you, this type can also be liken to you working offline for your boss and get your pay every month end, your boss can decide to fire you any day and that is it. The money stop coming once you are fired.

This type of income comes quicker and in bulk, it pays the rent, takes care of your immediate needs and keeps you happy, but is not recurring, ones you mismanaged it, is gone and you have to work again to keep the smile on your face.

Now, the passive income: this type of income don't come in bulk, it comes little by little but it doesn't stop coming, in this type of income, you only work once and once is enough, this income never stop coming but is not large that will make you want to mad shopping, but in time, in the future it will make you a millionaire or even a billionaire. With passive income, you make money even when you are sleeping.

So that is why I work for the two, active income for my immediate need, passive income for my future needs.

So are we clear now? Okay, let's move on

Types of active income:

- Exclusive contract, they pay you for the work done and that is it.
- Buying and selling
- Working for your boss in the office etc.

Types of passive income :

- non- exclusive contract
- You own the right to your business
- You keep making money even when you sleep, and it never stop flowing even to your next generation.
- It never stop flowing until it over flows and run down to water your garden.

Now for the sake of this ebook, I'm going to be talking only on passive income, what they are and how you can start on your way to making those passive income.

If you are ready to start then let's go.

For you to make this money online, you must and most importantly have a phone, laptop, Internet connection and the willingness to make your first $200 online and I believe that you are ready, for you to buy this book means that you are more than ready to start making those money.

If you have this three things in place, then let's set you up to the right direction.

DIFFERENT THINGS YOU NEED TO TRY NOW.

Now this are the things that make people money online

anywhere in the world, it doesn't matter which country you are reading this from, the same method and approach will get you the same result.

Those who make money online are doing:

1: Writing Books, fiction and non-fiction

2: Blogging

3: Gaming

4: Youtube

5: Buying and selling online etc.

And you can do all this things from the comfort of your home.

Now mind you, this things are capable to transforming your life forever, they are going to be making you a millionaire as you bring out yourself to do them.

The only thing I want from you is your undivided attention.

Note: you don't have to do all at once, as it will not allow you to make much progress. So my advice is to start with one, and then when you master one, you can then move to the next one.

That been said, since you buy this book from me, let me be

open to you.

You bought this book, so I might ask well be open to you so you don't make the same mistake I make when I was starting out.

If you are starting out with no money just like me, and you only have just your phone or laptop, then please ignore every other thing for now and focus on first item listed above, which is writing books, either fiction or non-fiction, this is where you will start making tons of money that if care is not taken you will ignore everything else, and focus on that.

And in a few minutes I'm going to show you where you can sell this books that you've just written and the money will start coming to you.

Now if you don't know what fiction and non-fiction books is, don't worry I will tell you.

Fiction are story books like fantasy, Romance, werewolf, etc.

Example of fictional books

1: In love with your sister

2: The girl is mine

3: Love out of league

4: You can't have me

5: Agent Q (The Mafia Boss series)

6: Princes of Troy

All this are my books and you can click on the links to check out how they are written and follow that pattern to create your first fantasy novel.

Now this five books has earned me 3 million naira as at the time of writing this ebook, mind you, I was broke with no money in my account, living in an uncompleted building then all of a sudden I have N3, 000,000.00 in my account using just my phone, at that time I didn't have laptop, it was later that I bought one Lenovo laptop.

Writing novels are cheap ways to make tons of money into your account on monthly basis.

People love reading love stories and will pay any amount you sell just to read your write up.

Now you may say that you are not an author and as such can not write.

My dear, authors are not born, they are made. I was not anywhere near the title author when I started, you can read my books above and you will see that my first books have lots of mistakes but I kept pushing, if I will make money then to hell with anything that will stop me.

I am not an English student, in fact I have C in English and trust me, I can't even defend it, but that is not my problem, my problem is to make money and that is what is pushing me to get better in writing.

So the second type of books you can write is non-fiction, just like this one you are reading now, this book is not a fantasy book, you can't imagine anything here, this book is based on facts and reality of life, you can't fake it here, you write what you know and have experienced, you write about what you have handle and is working for you, you can write about cars, how to take care of dogs, how to keep a man, how to make your woman happy, how to treat malaria at home, how to make money online, how to rent your car, how to fall in love with the right person, etc.

What ever life experience you have, you can put it in writing and sell it off to the general public.

Funny enough, you don't know how many people are willing to pay for your information.

So that is the first thing you need to do, in other to start making money almost immediately.

Why I'm emphasizing on this is because so that you don't go wasting your time on the internet doing things that won't pay you and in the long run you say is not working.

If you are in urgent need of money, write a book and sell it online to the platforms I will be listening for you shortly.

You can use this platforms to make passive income and active income, it will change your life for good.

Now that been said, start now, and write your first chapter of your novel using Microsoft word, you can download it from your playstore on any of your Android device. And you can start writing novels or ebooks.

For me novels are easy because you really don't need to be right or wrong, you just write anything that pop up in your head, it didn't necessary need to be true story, in fact, is the imagination of your mind that you will be using to make money, and your mind is unlimited, you can imagine anything and write them down turning them into a beautiful love story and your money keeps flowing.

As a matter of fact, writing this ebook is the hardest thing for me comparing to writing a novel.

I can now write a 400 chapters novel without getting tired but this ebook has only 50 pages, not chapters but I can tell you, is hard to put all this in place.

THINGS YOU NEED TO WRITE YOUR FIRST BOOK AND MAKE MONEY.

1: You will be needing your phone or laptop

2: You will need to install Microsoft Word on them.

3: You will need an internet connection

4: You will need a platform to sell your books to them or they help you sell your books for a royalty fee.

5: You will need a cover page for your books

6: You will need a little knowledge on how to type with a phone or laptop, hahaha.

Now after you have all this in place, you need to write your first book, then is time to make money.

PLATFORMS THAT WILL PAY YOU FOR YOUR BOOKS.

This platforms will either pay you as an exclusive contract or non-exclusive contract.

In the beginning of this book I've talked about passive and active income, this is what I meant, so if you are still asking questions about what is exclusive and non-exclusive, I will advise you go back at the beginning and read again.

So with that said, you will be choosing between exclusive and non-exclusive contract, they will review your book and if it meets their standard, they will contact you to sign a contract with them.

Exclusive contract is like this, they will pay you off, and the book will become their own forever, you no longer have any right over the books. But you will have your money in bulk, you can go buy what ever you want to buy with your money and live the good live, if you write as many as ten books on exclusive contract and you plan your income very well, then you can use the rest to write for non-exclusive.

But apart from this platforms you can also sell your books yourself and keep all the money.

I will show you all that, just keep reading and if you are getting any value on this book, please recommend it to all your friends and family members.

And you can subscribe to my [YouTube channel here.](#)

So let's continue.

Non-exclusive contract, you have the right to your books and you can still earn Royalty from the same companies for the rest of your life but this money comes in bit and pieces for example.

You could earn something like $0.7 if you have little readers.

Some of my books I earn somewhere around $7.0, $35.3, $7.6 I even earn $0.7 on one of my book (Princess of Troy,) the book is very short and that is why the amount is small. On revenue share.

But when it comes to my other books that I put a lot of effort like (The girl is mine, and In love with your sister) I earn somewhere around $35.0 dollars in passive income that is revenue share. apart from the main money that they already pay me in active income.

Like I earn in active income from my book in love with your sister around $1350 converting that to my own currency it give me N675, 000.00 at the time.

The dollar is not steady so I use the rate at that time.

Making such money is a miracle to me for just one book, is a dream come through for someone who don't have a house to sleep in. Hmmm.

Now let's head over to how you can do this yourself.

1: First thing first.

Write your book either fiction or nonfiction, you know the one that suit you best.

2: Design a cover page.

3: go to this apps and website and create an account with them.

APPS NAME TO MAKE MONEY WRITING.

- Light Reader app
- Webnovel App
- Wattpad
- Dreame
- Amazon KDP
- Paperwiff etc.

There are lots of them out there but know this, is not for you to join all of them that matters, what matters is that you are making money hence one or two of the platform is enough.

As for me, I use Light Reader app, they are the best for starters, if you have never written a book before and you just want to start and make money, use light reader app to start, they are the app I use to make over 2.4 million and I'm still there making money till date. My contract with them is going to expire in 50 years time so you see, they are going no where, join now, and start, you don't need any investment to make money there, they are all free.

Amazon KDP.

I will advise you to start writing with light reader before you move to Amazon KDP or to Webnove as the two place required high level excellent. What I meant is this.

You may find some spelling errors on light reader and they will still accept your books, but not with webnover or KDP.

So start with light reader, make your millions and then move on to KDP and Webnovel when you are familiar with the writing community then you can make more millions that will make you a billionaire. Does that make sense?.

THINGS YOU NEED TO CREATE ACCOUNT WITH LIGHT READER APP

1: Your phone

2: Your Bank account details

3: Your National Identification Number

Note: they are not accepting Voters Card so get your National identity Card ready before you apply if not you will have a problem.

After you create your account, upload the first chapter of your book and cover page where is necessary and hit publisher, they will give you a number of words you need to upload before someone will contact you and send you a contract to sign.

HOW TO UPLOAD YOUR BOOKS ON AMAZON KDP

The way you upload on KDP is not the same way you upload on Light reader, light reader is more simple than KDP

In KDP you need to format your book in sizes and format, and you need to upload the whole book at once.

While in light reader and order platform you only upload chapters by chapters and you only have 27 days to upload in a month to get your daily update bonus of $200 every month is that simply.

So you get $200 dollars every month till you finished the book.

Lets say you finished the book in four months you will receive $200x4. = $800 convert it to naira you get N400,000 pulse your completion bonus of let's say $400 depending on how long your story is, you now have $800+$400 = $1200 on one book then convert again you have N600,000.00 in one book. That is for active income.

Now after you collect all that money, you will still get revenue share every month from…. Something like $35.00 or $17.00 depending on how many people are reading your book.

****

I hope you understand all I have explained about writing your own books and selling them online.

If you have any questions you want to ask concerning how to write your own e-books and novel, send me a mail @ beautyisrael5@gmail.com

Now mind you, I have lots of emails coming through to me, so make your subject very clear so I will reply you quick, if I don't reply you on your first mail, send another one, it may be that your mail has been mixed up with other mail.

E.g give your mail a title like: HOW TO WRITE AN EBOOK.

And then State what you want, that way, I will know you are coming from this ebook and I will reply you asp.

That is all for writing your books and selling them online and making tons of money, and yes, one more thing, did I tell you that even though you can't write your own book, there are website that will help you out?

You heard me right, there are website that you can download free ebooks on any topic of your choice and edit them to your name, this ebook are totally free and have no copyright claim, meaning you can download them for free and sell them and keep the money to yourself, I made a short video on how you can do that, click on the link here and watch that video, it has the full details of how to download the books, the name of the websites, I want you to get it right the first time that is why I create video to support my clams.

Now that been said, you can decide to do it yourself if you think you have a specific massage to pass across to the public and you don't need another person idea, that's total good, at least you have the self esteem to tell someone I wrote this book myself, and you will be happy about yourself.

Like this ebook you are reading now, I took my time to write it because I have a message and the experience that I wanted to pass across to the public.

THE SECOND ONLINE BUSINESS YOU NEED TO START IS:

BLOGGING:

Blogging is another way people make money online, take away blogging and you don't have the Internet, everything you go to the internet to find is other peoples blogs.

If there are no bloggers, there will be no internet.

If you are looking for how to make money online, for example, the web will take you to someone's blog that has the type of information you are looking for, if no body has a blog on the internet, you may not likely to find what you are looking for.

So people make money by blogging and anytime you visit a particular blog, the owner of the blog make money, either by Google ads or by referrer links.

And that money he or she is making is passive money.

And that is why I said if you are starting out with no money, the first business to do is write a book, it will give you money faster, the blog will give you money but it takes time, you have to get what is call traffic to your blog before you will start to make money.

And sometimes getting those traffic is hard. But once you get your traffic, there is nothing that will stop you from making tons of passive income, money that you no longer work for, they just keep coming as long as you have your website up there.

Which brings us to the types of blogs you can create.

There are two types of blogs.

1: pay website

2: Free website

Pay website is the website that you pay for hosting and domain name. Meaning you choose a plan to pay to host your website, you can pay for one year or two.

The free website is the one that you don't have to pay a dime to host and domain name.

Now mind you, the free hosting website have lots of limitations, they can't be compared to the pay website, like for example on the free hosting platform you get low traffic, limited access to your website and lots of other limited, that been said, it doesn't mean you won't make money from the free website, but I hardly see someone who do

Back in 2015 you can make tons of money with a free bloggerspot but now, it's no longer easy, you have to buy hosting on either Namecheap, GoDaddy, Hostgator, Bluehost etc. To start having traffic almost immediately that your website go live, but for you that is starting new, I think you should use the free hosting platform to familiarize yourself with the blogging environment before you go ahead to buy hosting and domain name.

As for me I took years to build and design on free web hosting platform that today won't take me 5 minutes to build one, but my love for writing books has made me to stop creating blogs because I don't have time for it again.

If you want to see one of my blog click on this link.

I created this blog to showcase my books and I added the links to my books on the blog post, so that if anyone should click on the link, it will direct the person to my books in light reader where they will go and read my books.

And if you look very well on this free blog, there is a button to earn money as people visit the blog.

You can earn money by google ads on this free blogger spot.

So if you don't have money to buy a hosting and domain name, you can simply start off with a free blog and start to earn money every month with your free blog.

CAN YOU MAKE MONEY WITH A FREE BLOG?

My answer is yes! You can make money using a free blog, the only problem you will have is getting lots of traffic to your blog, that is getting people to visit your blog more often. And the only way to do that is to write about what people will love to read, if they like your content, they will come for more, if they don't like what you put out there, they might likely not come back for more.

HOW TO GET TRAFFIC TO YOUR BLOG:

There are tons of way to get traffic to your blog,

1: use your social media to get traffic to your blog

2: use paid promotion to get traffic to your blog.

3: very important, use SEO to get traffic to your blog.

4: Use social media influencers to get traffic to your blog. Not recommended for someone who is starting new, and especially if you don't have the money to.

That is why I recommend you start with writing books, that is where you get money without buying anything and you will see the money rolling in.

I can't say this enough, I smile to the bank every month, and that is how it suppose to be.

GAMING

The next best way people make money online is through games, they play games to win, some create the games, if you think you can play to win then good for you, and if you think that you like game too much, you can create them by yourself and sell it out to the public, anytime people download your game app and plays, you get paid.

But that requires a lot of work and is not suitable for someone like us who needs urgent money to sort out our bills.

But the truth is, if you love gaming, you can give it a try, there are lots of apps and website out there that will get you started.

YOUTUBE CHANNEL

Here is another way to create a passive income.

I know that you know what YouTube is, but have you create one for yourself? If you have not done so, then you are doing yourself more harm than good.

Youtube is a way for creating money for the future, it won't come so fast, but when it does start, it keeps coming and you began to blame yourself for not started earlier.

Now tell me how you will feel if you wake up one morning and find $10,000 in ads revenue in your account and that money just keeps increase every month?

And worse thing is that you don't have to buy anything to start creating videos on YouTube, all I use to create my own videos are my smartphone, I use it to record, edit, upload to YouTube and people finds it and watch them.

Good thing is once you create a video, is for life, you don't have to do anything else, one of your video could earn you lots of money in the future.

For you to know how much people make monthly on YouTube, you should check others out on the internet, there are lots of people who are willing to share their income record to the public, that way, you will get a glimpse of what you are about to enter.

I have been following Patricia Bright on youtube and other YouTubers, and all I just wanted was to be like them and be able to tell people how much I've been making too, so I started my own channel cup of co tv. Clink on link to see it.

When I started I was so desperate to get subscribers and views, I thought it will be easy but believe me you, I almost get discouraged with the slow growth of that channel, I never believed I could get up to 330 subscribers.

It was so discouraging but since I make money with my books on Amazon and light reader, I just keep pushing as I know that one day, I will get my channel to the promise land.

WHAT YOU NEED TO START A YOUTUBE CHANNEL

All the things you need to start a YouTube channel are available to you free but not all,. They are :

1: A Gmail account. -Free of charge

2: Your smartphone or camera

3: A ring light which serves both as tripod and light

4: A youtube channel- free of charge

5: Create videos on any topic and upload

6: Upload at least 100 videos

7: Get your channel to 1000 subscribers

8: Get your channel to 4,000 watch hour

9: Join the YouTube partnership program a.k.a Google ads and start making those cool dollars

All this things may seem hard at first, but if your eyes are on the prize you will keep going and never gets tired.

Let me tell you how I keep pushing.

I have a vision of making my first N27,000,000.00 on YouTube, that is $100,000.00 and that is how I keep pushing even though when it seems like nothing is working.

Whenever I looked at that goal, I just go back to work. So I encourage you to set a goal for yourself before you start your youtube channel, so when you start getting discourage, you can look at it and keep moving.

How much are you looking at to make from YouTube? Are you willing to make it your long time career or you just want to go in and come out?

Choose for yourself what is that you really want out of your channel and keep making videos that will bring people back to your channel.

HOW MUCH CAN I MAKE WITH YOUTUBE CHANNEL?

It depends on how big your channel is, but if you are starting new, don't set your expectations too high, because you may get discouraged when you find out that for a whole year, after been monetize, you still haven't made $100, but the twist is, you will wake up one morning and a miracle has happened to you and that is it.

So my advice is, write books, sell them on Amazon and light

reader, start your YouTube channel and wait for it to grow, you might just be a millionaire before you know it.

BONUS TIPS

How to get books to sell for free without writing them yourself

How to sell other peoples product and make money

How to re-upload other people's videos on your YouTube channel and make money fast., free of charge.

If you are reading this book and you think that you don't have the talent to do any of this things like writing your own book or creating your own youtube videos from scratch. Don't worry, didn't I promise you that I will teach you how to make your first $200?.

Just relax, is by fire by force, you must start making money today, just follow the instructions in this e-book, and you will be on your way to getting those money.

I will show you the website that you can go and download this copyright free e-book on any topic of your choice, all you need to do is download them onto your PC, edit them to your name and boom, you will start making money.

I will also show you how to upload your first book to Amazon KDP. Just click this link to watch the video.

Haven't said that, let's go with the first one. **HOW TO GET BOOKS TO SELL FOR FREE WITHOUT WRITING THEM YOURSELF**

HOW TO GET BOOKS TO SELL FOR FREE WITHOUT WRITING THEM YOURSELF

Publish Books Written by Someone Else

So what this means for you is that you can take any public domain work and republish it for profit! It's that simple, is legal to republish someone else's work in this way, and many people are making good money doing it! Here are a few resources you can use to get started after you read this book.

Can You Legally Sell Public Domain Content?

Selling works without a copyright is perfectly legal. Although copyright laws can be somewhat confusing, there are some basic guidelines you can refer to:

- In the US, any book published before 1923 is considered to be in the public domain.
- Books published in 1923 or later are in the public domain if the copyright was not renewed.
- A public domain book can be used freely, reformatted, reprinted, and sold anywhere you like.

How to Find Public Domain Books

However, figuring out whether or not a book has a current copyright or not can be a little tricky. Probably the **best place to locate books without a copyright is Project Gutenberg**. You can also use this comprehensive **list of public domain book sources** to find what you're looking for.

How to Publish a Public Domain Book

By far, the best place to publish a public domain work is on Amazon. and **Kindle Direct Publishing (KDP)** for the Kindle format. By the way, you can **publish your own original books** for sale on these sites too!

When you create an account at one or both of these sites, you will be guided through every step to publish your first book.

Below are some general directions on *how to get your book published* through KDP.

Pick a Book Title

There are thousands of public domain books to choose from. Go to GutenbergProject or do a Google search using a title you're already familiar with or a search term for a subject you're interested in.

Make sure you're able to get the full text of the book before you go any further.

Format the Book

Check out all the text in your book. Make sure the formatting is correct:

- Check that the heading for each chapter is in the proper place.
- Check for any major spelling errors.
- Make sure the Table of Contents is correct.

- Generate a linked table of contents using your favorite text editing tool.

Create a Cover for Your Book

If you're handy with design on the computer, you can create a book cover yourself. Otherwise you can hire someone else to create a book cover for you. Unless you know someone who will do it for free, hiring someone will cost you a hundred bucks or more.

However, hiring a professional can be a good move if they can create a cover that draws attention and helps drive sales.

Convert The Text to the Kindle Format

When setting up your book for sale in the Kindle store, you'll need to format it for the Kindle platform. Amazon provides a free tool to help you do that.

The Kindle Generator will help you convert your cover art, table of contents, and text into a mobile format the Kindle hardware can display properly.

Finishing Touches

Once you have everything converted to the Kindle format, then you can finish the job and post your book to the Kindle store.

You'll need to:

- Write a great description that will compel customers to buy the book.
- Generate keywords that make your book searchable in the Kindle store.
- Set the price for your book.

It usually takes Amazon about 24-48 hours to post your book in the store once you hit publish. You can start making money in no time!

How You Get Paid for Your Public Domain Book

Each time someone purchases your book on Amazon, you get 35% of the sale price. You'll be paid monthly for your efforts. Of course, the more books you have in the store and the more you promote them, the more you'll sell!

How to Sell More Books

One of the best things you can do when you publish a public domain book is to differentiate your book from others in the store with the same title.

Amazon encourages this by requiring you add value to set your book apart from the rest. If someone already has a free version of your book in the store, you can't charge for it unless you have some type of added value attached. There are several ways you can add value:

- Add a biography of the author.
- Additional research into the history of the book.

- Original illustrations.
- Annotations
- Commentaries

How Much Can You Earn?

How much can you earn selling public domain books? Well, that depends on you! Your earnings will depend on several factors:

- The titles you choose- some will be more popular than others.
- The number of books you have for sale. The more titles you have available, the more you will sell overall.
- How much you promote each book.

Overall, you can make anywhere from $100-$200 per month up to thousands of dollars depending on the factors above.

There are even some people who make a full time living this way!

How Difficult is it to Get Started?

Getting started with public domain publishing is not extremely hard. However, the process of finding a good title and setting everything up can be a little technical.

But if you're used to using a computer, you should be able to get the job done and **start making money**! Just like anything, the more times you do it, the easier it gets!

How to Make Money Selling Other People's Products

Today, a lot of people make money from online sales. In fact, every time you go on social media, someone is sharing the story of how they have been able to make huge sums of money from selling other people's products.

But why would people choose to sell other people's products instead of their own? Well, it can be difficult to develop your own product. You also don't know if it will be successful. That means you would be taking a risk that might not even generate profit. But with selling other people's products, such risks do not exist. The products have been verified and market proven. All you just have to do is sell the product and profit through commissions. Here are four ways you can do that.

Becoming a Sales Representative

Sales representatives are people who sell products and earn a percentage of the sales as their commission. The commission is directly related to the amount of products they sell. The more they sell, the more profit they make. There are quite a number of organizations that are offering online affiliate or sales programs that allow people to sell their products and earn commission on them.

Drop-Shipping

Drop-shipping is mostly an online type of selling. The seller facilitates the purchase of a product from the producer. The product is delivered directly to the buyer without the seller touching the product. However, they get a cut of the transaction for facilitating the deal. Drop-shipping removes the hidden cost of running an inventory shop. You also don't have to hire employees. You don't have to buy and store before you sell.

Drop-shipping also allows you to start with a little amount of money. This makes it very easy for anyone to join.

What Is Affiliate Marketing and How To Get Started

This complete guide will walk you through how to start making money in **affiliate marketing**, with online marketing tips and tricks to help you earn more money.

Smart entrepreneurs running a thriving business know there's always more they can do to make that business grow. One way of taking things to the next level is by finding an alternate stream of income.

What is affiliate marketing?

Affiliate marketing is a process where publishers earn a commission by promoting a product or service made by another retailer or advertiser. The affiliate partner is rewarded a payout for providing a specific result to the retailer or advertiser.

Typically, the result is a sale. But some programs can reward you for leads, free-trial users, clicks to a website, or getting downloads for an app.

Affiliate programs are usually free to join, so you don't have to worry about high startup costs. Done well, this performance-based opportunity can go from side hustle to profitable online business idea by netting you a healthy income.

How affiliate marketing works

Affiliate marketing involves referring a product or service by sharing it on a blog, social media platform, podcast, or website. The affiliate earns a commission each time someone makes a purchase through the unique link associated with their recommendation.

To review:

1. You show an ad or a link for Store Z on your website, blog, or social network.
2. A customer clicks your unique link.
3. The customer makes a purchase in Store Z.
4. The affiliate network records the transaction.
5. The purchase is confirmed by Store Z.
6. You get paid a monetary commission.

Commission rates vary depending on the company and the offer. On the low end, you'll earn about 5% of the sale but, with some arrangements, you can earn as much as 50%, usually when promoting a class or event. There are also affiliate marketing programs that provide a flat rate per sale instead of a percentage.

Types of affiliate marketing

Affiliates always carry a bit of mystery—you never know if the person has ever *really* used the product, or if they are just promoting it for the money. Both cases still exist today.

It wasn't until 2009 when renowned affiliate marketer Pat Flynn broke down the different types of affiliate marketers into three groups. Understanding these types of affiliate marketing can show you the different ways people **make money online** in this space, regardless of your moral compass.

Unattached

The first type of affiliate marketing is referred to as "unattached," or when you have no authority in the niche of the product you're advertising. There is no connection between you and the customer. Often you are running pay-per-click advertising campaigns with your affiliate link and hoping people will click it, buy the product, and earn a commission.

Unattached affiliate marketing is attractive because you don't need to do any legwork. Affiliate marketing businesses rely on reputation and trust with a target audience online. Some don't have the time or desire to build those relationships, so this type of marketing is their best option.

"Unattached affiliate marketing isn't a genuine business model, it's for people who just want to generate income," explains Elise Dopson, founder of Sprocker Lovers. "Our focus for Sprocker Lovers is building community and providing free education around a particular niche first, which in our case is the sprocker spaniel dog breed, and selling second."

Related

Related affiliate marketing is where you promote products and services you don't use, but that are related to your niche. Affiliates in this case have an audience, whether it's through blogging, YouTube, TikTok, or another channel. They have influence, which makes them a trusted source for recommending products, even if they've never used it before.

The problem with related affiliate marketing is, do you want to promote something you've never tried before? It could be the worst product or service ever and you wouldn't even know. It only takes one bad recommendation to lose the trust of your audience. If you don't have trust and transparency, it'll be hard to build a sustainable affiliate marketing business.

Involved

Involved affiliate marketing refers to only recommending products and services you've used and truly believe in. "Involved affiliate marketing is the way forward," says Elise. "It's rooted in trust and authenticity, which is best for your audience and business."

In this type of marketing, you use your influence to promote products and services that followers may actually need, instead of paying to get clicks on a banner ad. It takes more time to build this type of credibility with an audience, but it's necessary to build a sustainable business.

Elise explains that advertising also becomes much easier. "You don't have to hide behind expensive PPC ads and hope for clicks and sales. An organic Instagram Story or blog post about your experience with a product will go a long way." Elise prefers this method because it's honest and is "the only genuine way to become a trusted source on any topic."

Pros and cons of affiliate marketing

Pros

Yes, affiliate marketing is worth it, given its growth in popularity. Statista estimates the affiliate marketing industry will be worth $8.2 billion by 2022, up from $5.4 billion in 2017. It's also a low- to no-cost business venture you can profit from immensely.

While industry growth is a good indication of success, entrepreneurs also take this **referral marketing** route for a few other reasons.

Easy to execute

Your side of the equation simply involves handling the digital marketing side of building and selling a product. You don't have to worry about the harder tasks, like developing, supporting, or fulfilling the offer

Low risk

Since there's no cost to join affiliate programs, you can start making money with an established affiliate product or service without any upfront investment. Affiliate marketing also can generate relatively **passive income** through commission—the ideal money-making scenario. Though initially you'll have to invest time creating traffic sources, your affiliate links can continue to deliver a steady paycheck.

Easy to scale

Successful affiliate marketing offers the potential to significantly scale your earnings without hiring extra help. You can introduce new products to your current audience and build campaigns for additional products while your existing work continues to generate revenue in the background.

Before you get too excited, know that great affiliate marketing is built on trust. While seemingly there is an endless number of products or services to promote, it's best to only highlight those you personally use or would recommend. Even when a product interests you or fits within an existing hobby, becoming a great marketer for that product takes a lot of work.

Cons

Affiliate marketing also has a few disadvantages compared to other platforms. Before jumping in, let's look at a few challenges you'll face on your journey to success.

Requires patience

Affiliate marketing is not a get-rich-quick scheme. It requires time and patience to grow an audience and gain influence.

You'll want to test different channels to see which connect best with your audience. Research the most relevant and credible products to promote. And spend time blogging, publishing free content on social media, hosting virtual events, and doing other lead-generating activities.

Commission-based

There's no boss handing you a weekly paycheck as an affiliate marketer. Affiliate programs work on a commission basis, whether you're paid by lead, click, or sale.

Companies use a temporary browser cookie to track peoples' actions from your content. When a desired action is taken by someone, you receive the payout.

No control over program

Affiliates must obey the rules set by a company for their program. You need to follow their guidelines for what you say and how you present their product or service. Competitors must follow the same recommendations, so you have to get creative to differentiate yourself from the crowd.

How do affiliate marketers make money?

Affiliate marketing income spans a large spectrum. There are some marketers that'll make a few hundred bucks per month and others that make six figures a year. The larger your following, the more money you can make.

Compensation software company Payscale reports that the average annual salary of an affiliate marketer is $52,130, based on over 7,000 salary profiles, with the highest tier making an annual salary of $72,000.

There are also marketers like blogger Ryan Robinson, who makes over $17,000 per month through affiliate income alone. This image below shows Ryan's blog income for March 2021:

But how do affiliates actually get paid? When you choose an affiliate program to promote, you'll notice there are different payment models. Companies also call it a price model, payout model, conversion type, or another variation.

Regardless of the name, the payment model tells you what goals you will get paid for. If you're promoting a software product, the action could be a free trial signup. For marketers that promote physical products, the goal will likely be a purchase.

Many programs run with last-click attribution, which means the affiliate who receives the last click before purchase gets 100% credit. However this is changing, as programs improve attribution models and reporting. For example, you could share equal credit for a sale if there were multiple affiliates in a buyer's conversion funnel.

Five common ways affiliates get paid include:

- **Pay per sale,** where you earn a commission for each sale you make. It's a common payout model for ecommerce offers.

- **Pay per action,** which earns you a commission for a specific action. Many affiliate programs use this payout model because it's broad and can be applied to different offers: a newsletter signup, a click, contact request, form submission, etc.

- **Pay per install**, where you are paid for every install generated from your website traffic. The goal of your content would be to promote mobile apps and software so that people download or install them.

- **Pay per lead,** which pays you every time someone signs up for something. It's a popular payout method because companies use it for sweepstakes, lead generation, and other types of offers. Cost per lead offers are common for beginners because it's easier to generate leads than to sell products to an audience.

- **Pay per click,** a rare payout system where you earn commission on every click on your affiliate link. Pay per click programs are used by big merchants with a goal to build brand awareness. Customers don't need to sign up or buy anything, just to visit the merchant's website.

How much you make depends on your affiliate niche. For example, our research* found that the highest average commission rate ($70.99) was for business-related programs. While books and media and clothing categories earned just over $6 per commission. The maximum average commission we found was around $289.06 per sale.

How to start affiliate marketing in 4 steps

Here is how to start affiliate marketing:

1. Pick your platform and method
2. Decide your niche and audience
3. Find your products
4. Choose your first affiliate program

Just like running your own small business, becoming a successful affiliate takes dedication and discipline. Use the following step-by-step guide to start your affiliate marketing business.

Pick your platform and method

The first step is figuring out the platform you want to build your audience around. Every affiliate marketer has a different approach and platform. There are many affiliate marketing ideas you can choose from based on different methods:

- **Niche topic and review sites.** These are sites that review products for a specific audience or compare a line of products against their competitors. This method requires you to create content related to the review space and post regularly to draw in an audience.

- **Digital content.** Digital content creators include bloggers, YouTubers, or social media influencers. They create niche content that resonates with a target audience. The goal is to organically introduce niche products their audience will enjoy. This increases the chances they'll buy and you'll earn an affiliate commission.

- **Courses, events, workshops.** If you're an educator, you can integrate affiliate partnership offers into your events.

No matter which route you take, authenticity and audience building are the two most crucial elements for affiliate marketing.

To pick a platform and method, ask yourself:

- What platforms do you use the most?
- Which platforms do you understand best?

Common platforms affiliate marketers use are:

- Blogging
- Instagram
- TikTok
- Facebook
- Pinterest
- Pay per click (PPC)

Starting with a marketing platform you're comfortable with helps you create high-quality content. This can result in a stronger, more engaged audience you can turn into sales.

Decide your niche and audience

When it comes to choosing a niche, aim for something you're passionate and knowledgeable about. This helps you come across as authentic and as a trusted source of information for potential customers. It also helps you evaluate which products and brands you want to promote.

Say, for example, you started a blog about dogs. You own a sprocker spaniel and you're passionate about helping other owners care for their sprockers.

You create a blog like Sprocker Lovers, and you regularly post and encourage people to subscribe to an email list and share your content. Sprocker spaniels are your niche, and you're going to invest in content marketing and optimization to grow your audience of owners.

The niche you choose for your affiliate site guides how much time or effort you'll need to put into building it to a point where you begin to see SEO results," says Elise.

"SERPs for software, marketing, and health care, for example, are all dominated by huge blogging sites with even bigger marketing budgets. The secret is finding untapped areas where competition isn't as fierce—and getting in there before other people recognize it."

As you post more, you can use affiliate marketing devices like social listening tools, website analytics, and social media insights to discover who your audience is and what they like.

Remember, you're not paid to post. Affiliate marketing is a performance-based online business. If you know what your audience likes, you can then refer the best products to them and earn more affiliate income.

Find your products

To earn revenue as an affiliate marketer, your audience needs to connect with what you're saying. The items or services you promote need to be products they genuinely want. Getting this wrong can hinder your success and diminish your credibility—as well as your audience.

If you're curious where to look for products or brands to work with, don't worry. There are tons of affiliate marketplaces, including:

Another option is to visit the websites of the products and services you use and like to see if they have an affiliate program. Large companies often have programs they promote on their site, such as **Amazon Associates** or the **Shopify Affiliate Program**.

You also can take a more direct approach. Reach out to the owner of a great product you come across and see if they offer an affiliate marketing program. If they don't, they might be happy to set up an arrangement with you, such as offering you a special coupon code to share with your followers.

The best deals often are found when you're the first to inquire and have a relevant distribution channel, such as approaching the seller of a new fitness product if you're a health and wellness blogger.

Affiliate marketing programs will have terms of service you need to follow, so read the fine print. For example, your link usually will have a cookie with a specified timeframe, and some programs don't allow you to purchase pay-per-click ads using the product or company's name.

Choose your first affiliate program

As you brainstorm products or browse through affiliate platforms, the most important criteria to keep in mind is that the product should be aligned with your audience, or the audience you hope to build. Ask yourself, is it something your target audience would find valuable? Does it fit with your area of expertise?

A food blogger probably wouldn't promote beauty products, for example. A wide range of other products, such as cookware, meal kits, gourmet ingredients, or even aprons would make more sense.

Also make sure the product or service you're promoting is a fit for the platform you're promoting it on. For example, home décor and clothing are well suited to image-heavy platforms like **Instagram**. However, if you're promoting more in-depth purchases, like software, your conversion rates may be higher on longer-form platforms, like a blog or **YouTube**.

UPLOAD OTHER PEOPLE'S VIDEO AND MAKE MONEY

Yes you can get your own channel up and running even though you don't know how to create your own videos, there are platform that you can download their videos and reload to your channel free of charge.

Is all copyright free so you have the legal right to use them.

12 of the Best Free Stock Video Websites for Great Footage

People watch more than a billion hours of video on YouTube every day. Over on TikTok, more than a billion individual videos are viewed daily.

Even Instagram — the world's most popular photo-sharing app — has announced that its shifting its focus to video... probably because Instagram videos get twice the engagement of Instagram photos.
Overall, the average person spends about 100 minutes a day watching online videos.
The bottom line? Internet-using humans are *obsessed* with videos. Which means that video should be a vital part of your marketing or social campaign. (Wait, should this have been a video instead of an article? Excuse us while we have a quick spiral.)

But you don't need a professional videographer to create professional-grade video content for your marketing or social media accounts. You just need a good list of free stock video resources.

Which is exactly what we've got for you here. Read on for a list of websites for stock footage you can repurpose, remix or reimagine, without any stress about copyright infringement.

So grab the clips you need, and then add text, graphics or music to create highly watchable videos for your next marketing campaign… all for a sweet, sweet budget of zero dollars. Let's get to movie-making, shall we?

12 of the best sites for free stock videos

Pixabay

Pixabay offers over 2.3 million images and videos, all released under a simplified Pixabay License. All content on the site can be used for free, whether for commercial or non-commercial purposes, for print or digital. (Though certain downloads may specifically clarify "what is not allowed".) You don't need to get permission or give credit to the artist to use or modify the content, (but it's still best practice to always credit the owner). Pixabay has a great collection of HD stock videos, whether you're looking for a quick 12-second clip of someone typing or a minute-long shot of future earth from space.

Videvo

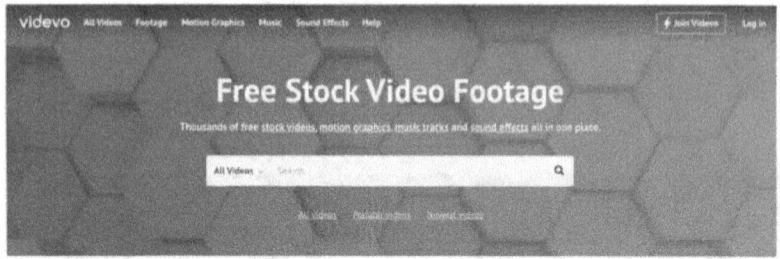

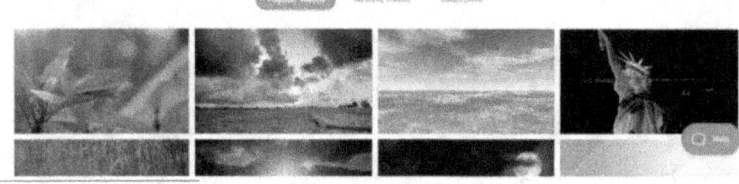

Videvo offers thousands of free stock video footage as well as motion graphics, music and sound effects created by their community of users.

The clips you download from Videvo will be licensed in a variety of different ways: some you may not be able to use for specific types of projects. There's a complete breakdown here of all the difference license types, but here's a quick summary:
- Videvo Attribution License allows you to use a clip for free, but you have to credit the original author.
- Clips with a Creative Commons 3.0 can also be used for free, with credit, and may be remixed or adapted.
- Public Domain licenses mean that they're yours to do with as you wish!

Check out the individual usage rights for each video for more details.

Pexels

Pexels began as a free photo site, but has since added a large library of free HD and 4K stock videos.

With Pexels' license, all photos and videos can be used for free, and without attribution (though giving credit to the videographer is certainly appreciated). Videos are OK to be edited and modified however you like.

Explore their daily "trending free stock videos" to find the most in-demand stock videos… like this soothing footage of hair being braided.

Videezy

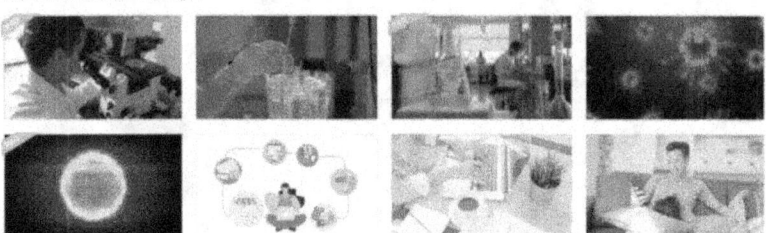

Videezy has a large collection of video clips that are royalty-free for personal and commercial use, but always make sure to check each clip's specific licensing info to make sure your favorite footage is available to use.

Most require that you credit Videezy.com when using their footage. However, you can also buy credits that will allow you to use footage without attribution.

There's a wide variety of high-quality video clips to choose from, in both HD and 4K resolution. When searching for videos, any results marked with "Pro" are premium clips that are only available by paying with credits.

Life of Vids

Life of Vids is a collection of free stock videos, clips, and loops from Leeroy, an advertising agency in Montreal, Canada. There are no copyright restrictions, but redistribution on other sites is limited to 10 videos. (If you feel so inclined, they welcome you to buy them a beer or give them a shoutout on your website.)

New videos are added weekly, and they've got a beautiful collection of free stock images you can check out as well.

Coverr

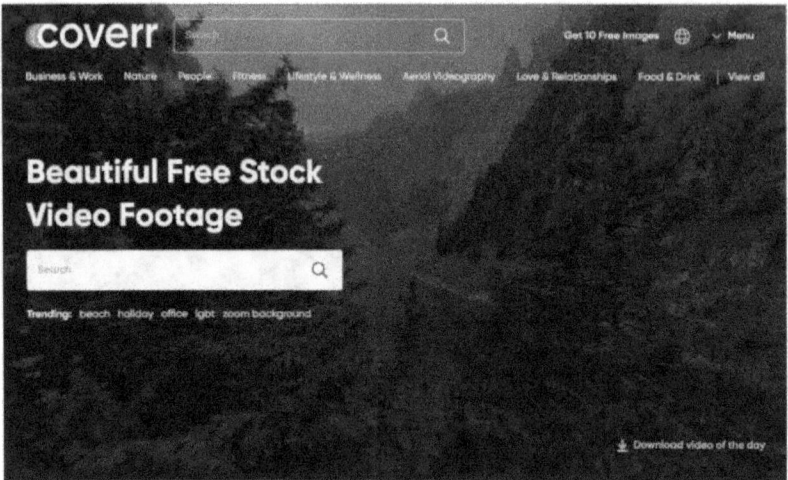

Started by entrepreneurs and filmmakers who needed good-looking video for their products, Coverr is intended to fill that same need for other up-and-coming brands: a little gift to the world, if you will.

Now, it has thousands of free videos, which have been downloaded more than five million times. All the videos are in HD, and available to download in MP4 format.

No sign-up needed, no attribution required, just instant downloads of free video footage. Use these sweet clips in commercial video projects or personal ones, and copy or modify them to your heart's content.

Splitshire

Splitshire was created by web designer Daniel Nanescu, who wanted to offer his photos and videos free for personal and commercial use. The fact that these photos and videos were all created by one person makes them more unique than content from other stock sites.

The videos are primarily drone footage of beautiful outdoor scenes, and you can download them by clicking on the title below each video. You're free to use them across all your social media channels, but you can't sell them or use them in projects with inappropriate content such as violence, racism, or discrimination.

Clipstill

Each month, Clipstill makes a handful of its web-quality "cinemagraphs" available for free download, so it's worth checking out and stocking up for future use. You never know when you're going to need some footage of a hot air balloon down the road, right?
If you don't want to wait around for just the right footage to come along (and have a few bucks to spare), you can also sign up for unlimited downloads for a one-time $49 fee.

Dareful

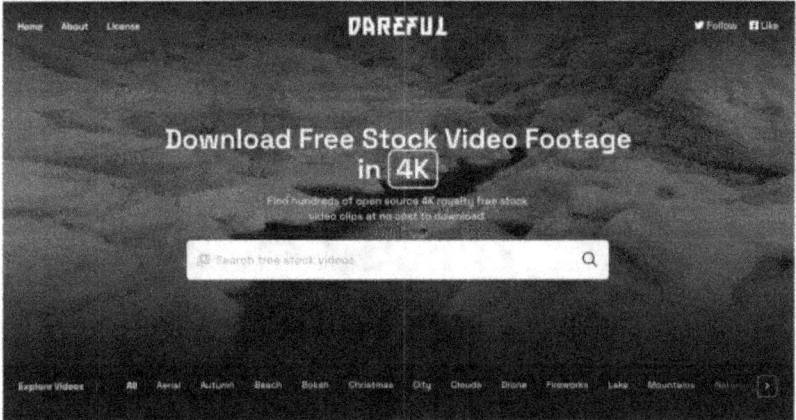

Okay, it's not a collection of thousands or millions of clips, but maybe there's something among the hundreds of open-source 4K royalty-free stock video clips here that will tickle your fancy.

Formerly known as Stock Footage for Free, Dareful provides stock footage that's licensed under Creative Commons 4.0, which means you're free to share and adapt as long as you give appropriate credit and indicate if any changes were made.
It's all shot by a videographer named Joel Holland. Why's he giving it all away? We may never know, but we can watch this time-lapse footage of ominous clouds as we ponder.

Vidsplay

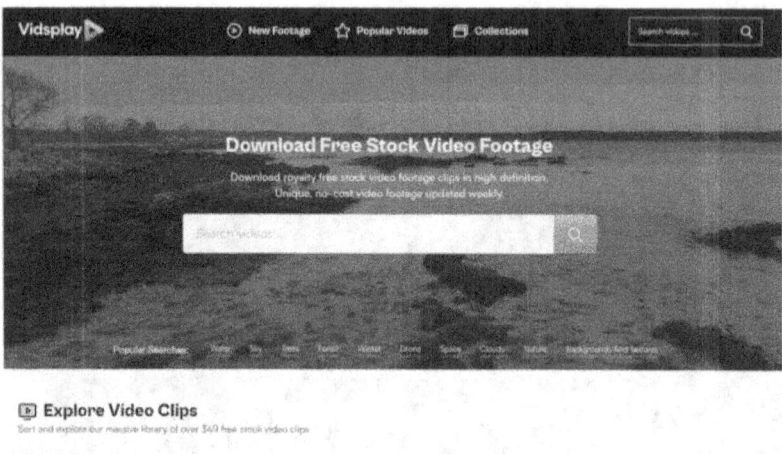

There are new videos added every few weeks to the Vidsplay collection, which makes it a great resource for keeping your social video content fresh. And since it's been around since 2010, there's a huge backlog of older content to pursue, too.

You can download and use any video without paying royalties, although you do need to provide attribution.

Mixkit

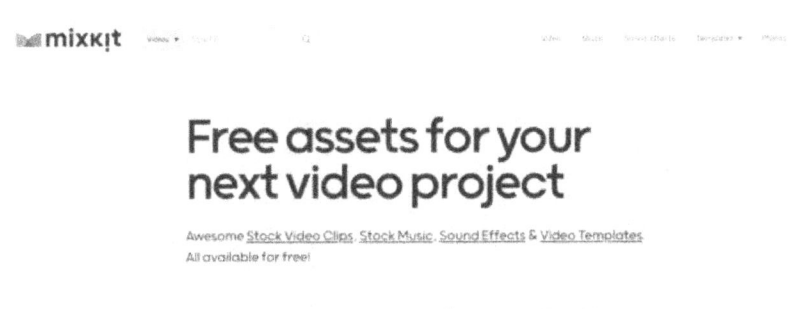

What can you stock your content coffers with over at Mixkit? We're talking stock video clips, sound effects, music and even video templates. It's a library of resources provided by a company called Envato, a subscription service for creative assets, but this batch is free, free, free, with new content being added every week, with no attribution required.

Mazwai

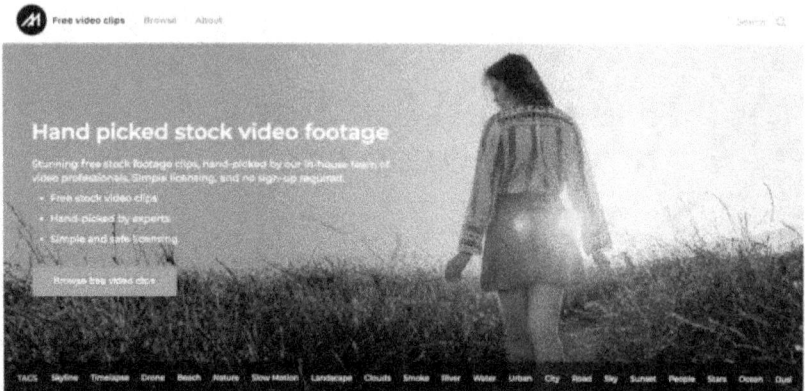

Mazwai describes its free stock footage and moving images as "hand-picked," though it doesn't really specify by who. But whatever mysterious forces are choosing the videos that wind up here for download, you're going to get high-definition content that's either licensed under the Creative Commons 3.0 license (use for whatever, just make sure to credit the author) or under the Mazwai License (use for whatever, no credit required).

Good luck to making your first $200 online, don't forget to leave a comment or review on the book

ABOUT THE AUTHOR

Beauty Israel is very good at making money online, she has been earning passive income from 2015 till date and is committed to helping people like you make money online.

What you will find inside this book are personal experience, on how she was able to scale up from $0 to making $5000 in passive income.

www.ingramcontent.com/pod-product-compliance
Lightning Source LLC
Chambersburg PA
CBHW071146240526
45465CB00024BA/1797